TEST YOUR NUMBER POWER

Michael Cornelius

WARD LOCK

A WARD LOCK BOOK

First published in the UK 1994
by Ward Lock Villiers House 41/47 Strand LONDON WC2N 5JE

A Cassell Imprint

Distributed in the United States
by Sterling Publishing Co., Inc.
387 Park Avenue South, New York, NY 10016-8810

Distributed in Australia
by Capricorn Link (Australia) Pty Ltd
2/13 Carrington Road, Castle Hill NSW 2154

A British Library Cataloguing in Publication Data block for this book
may be obtained from the British Library

ISBN 0 7063 7259 X
Design and typesetting Ben Cracknell
Illustrations John Headford

Printed and bound in Great Britain by Cox & Wyman

CONTENTS

INTRODUCTION

It is almost impossible to avoid numbers in our lives

What's the time?
What number bus do I need?
How much does that cost?
Which is my hotel room?
How many people will be coming?
They are offering me 10 per cent discount.
How old are you?
At what temperature do you want the oven set?
What was the final score?
How many days holiday do I have left?

We could all make long lists of situations that could not be easily resolved without the use of numbers, and we all use numbers without thinking and without worrying. Yet many of us panic when we are faced with a simple calculation. This book, therefore, offers some help for those who worry about number calculations. There is some practice in the form of tests – think of them as quizzes – and a few insights into the efficient use of a calculator as well as some helpful tips for short cuts and so on.

People have different motives for wanting to improve their numeracy skills. These days, many job applicants face numeracy tests from potential employers, while people in existing jobs often need improved fluency with numbers. A fear of numbers – and often a hidden sense of shame – is frequently carried over from school days. The often-heard 'I was never any good at mathematics' claim will often hide a feeling of inadequacy.

So, if you want to improve your skills with numbers or if you just enjoy the challenge of playing with numbers, this book should contain something of interest for you

Although you should use a calculator where necessary, there are many occasions when you can save time by using a little intelligence.

Estimating

Always try to estimate an answer first. You will then avoid producing answers that are obviously wrong. For example, if you are asked 'What is the cost of 27 articles at 18c each?' you should be thinking along the lines: 27×18 is near to 25×20, which is 500c or $5. So if you get an answer of, say, $12, $23 or 49c, something has gone wrong! The correct answer is, in fact, $4.86.

If the question is 'My bills for a month are £32.56, £45.80 and £79.37. What is the total I have spent?' you should be thinking of adding £30, £45 and £80 to get an estimate of £155. The correct answer is, in fact, £157.73. When it comes to percentages, you may be asked something like: 'An employee earning $12,450 is given a 10 per cent pay rise. What is the new salary?' Here you might argue that 10 per cent is one-tenth and one-tenth of $12,000 is $1,200 so the new salary will be something like $12,000 + $1,200 = $13,200. The correct answer is $13,695.

Do not be afraid to make estimates 'rough'. You make them so that you can assess whether or not an answer is 'sensible'.

Looking for Short Cuts

If you are faced with a list of figures to add – 'Add together 23, 57, 89, 45, 123 and 61', for instance – first look at the units digits and try to make 'tens'. Here, 3 + 7 = 10 and 9 + 1 = 10, leaving 5 + 3 = 8, so the units add up to 28. Now the tens digits: 2 + 8 = 10 and 4 + 6 = 10, leaving 5 + 12 = 17, giving a total of 370. Thus the final answer is 370 + 28 = 398.

Multiplication can sometimes be off-putting. Perhaps you will be asked to multiply 39 by 23. You should think that $40 \times 23 = 920$, so the answer is $920 - 23 = 897$.

A question on percentages might ask you to find 17.5% of $230: 10%, (one-tenth) = $23, 5% = $11.50 (divide $23 by 2), 2.5% = $5.75 (divide $11.50 by 2). Therefore, the required answer is $23 +$11.50 + $5.75 = $40.25.

Develop your own methods and short cuts. Although what is easy for one person does not always work for another, it is always useful to try to work in 'tens', 'hundreds' and so on.

Working Out Percentages

Have a look at a newspaper. You can almost guarantee that it will mention percentages in several places, and we all use the idea of percentages with great regularity:

I've got a 10 per cent pay rise.
Sale: 15 per cent off everything!
Inflation is now at 4.6 per cent.
45 per cent of the group were over 50.
Unemployment is up by 3.2 per cent.
15 per cent of cars are red.

Many people find great difficulty in working out calculations that involve percentages.

Remember that per cent means per hundred.

1% is one-hundredth, 5% is five-hundredths and so on. Therefore, 25% of 4,000 is 25-hundredths of 4,000, and we get this from: 25/100 × 4,000 = 1,000.

To increase something by a percentage we work as follows – for example, increase 560 by 12%. We want 112/100 × 560, so we calculate 1.12 × 560 = 627.2.

To increase 43 by 6% we want 106/100 × 43, so we calculate 1.06 × 43 = 45.58.

To decrease something by a percentage, we work as follows – for example, decrease 560 by 12%. We want 88/100 × 560, so we calculate 0.88 × 560 = 492.8.

To decrease 43 by 6%, we want 94/100 × 43, so we calculate 0.94 × 43 = 40.42.

Using Your Calculator

A calculator is a powerful aid, but it can only respond to your instructions! You will get the correct answers only if you feed in the correct information. This is why it is always worth estimating the expected size of the answer.

For example, if the question was 45.8×9.007, a sensible estimate would have been $45 \times 10 = 450$. The correct answer is 412.5206, but it is easy to get, say, 41.25206 by feeding in the wrong figures, say 4.58×9.007.

Experiment with the percentage key on your calculator. Try pressing it after 900×50, 400×25 and 600×75, you should get the answers 450, 100 and 450 – the calculator is working out the percentages for you.

Press the percentage key after $120 \div 240$, $50 \div 200$ and $36 \div 48$, and you should find you get the answers 50, 25 and 75. In each case the calculator is working out the first number as a percentage of the second.

Memories and Brackets
Use your calculator to work out $(4 \times 5)/(3 \times 7)$. Many people will calculate $4 \times 5 = 20$ and write down the answer; then work out $3 \times 7 = 21$ and write down the answer; before working out $20 \div 21 = 0.9523809$.

This is inefficient use of the calculator, because you do not need to write down intermediate steps. If your calculator has a memory try:

| 3 | x | 7 | = | M+ | C | 4 | x | 5 | = | ÷ | MR | = |

If your calculator has brackets try:

| (| 4 | x | 5 |) | ÷ | (| 3 | x | 7 |) | = |

Experiment with your calculator until you are fully aware of what it can do and how it operates.

THE PUZZLES

Each question begins with a note telling you whether a calculator is allowed and how much time you should allow.

All the answers are at the back of the book. Each puzzle has been cross-referenced with two numbers – a question number (Q) and an answer number (A). The answers are not in the same order as the questions so that when you look up the answers to one set of puzzles, there is no risk of seeing the answers to the next group before you have had an opportunity to tackle them.

The puzzles generally increase in difficulty as you progress through the book, but you may find some types are easier than others, even though they come later in the book. Some questions are of the 'multiple choice' type.

Do not be afraid to come back to a question to see if you can improve on an earlier mark. Keep a record of the times you take and see if you can improve both your speed and your accuracy.

If you score 80 per cent or more you are doing well and should keep moving on. If your score is below 40 per cent you need to brush up your number skills before rushing on!

Mental Practice 1

No calculator – 5 minutes

1. Add 57, 63 and 25.

2. Subtract 76 from 145.

3. Multiply 34 by 3.

4. Divide 360 by 8.

5. Find 30% of 900.

6. Increase 480 by 25%.

7. Decrease 480 by 25%.

8. Jack is twice as old as Jill who is 25 years younger than Janet. If Jack is 20, how old will Janet be in 5 years time?

9. How many minutes are there between 11.43 am and 1.15 pm?

10. How long will it take to travel 375 miles at 75 mph?

Mental Practice 2

No calculator – 5 minutes

1. Gasoline costs 59c per gallon. How much will 6 gallons cost?

2. Estimate $352.6 \div 50$ to the nearest whole number.

3. Find 7% of 850.

4. What is 140 as a percentage of 210?

5. What is one-tenth of 0.003?

6. At an exchange rate of $1.55 to £1, how many dollars will you get for £20?

7. Add together 17, 135, 25, 43 and 180.

8. A clock loses 3 minutes every hour. If it is correct at 1800, what time will it show at 0700 next morning?

9. A cup of coffee and a cup of tea cost $1 together. Two cups of coffee and three cups of tea cost $2.40. How much does one cup of coffee cost?

10. Add 3% of 200 to 5% of 700.

Mental Practice 3

No calculator – 5 minutes

1. Estimate 74.7×0.3 to the nearest whole number.

2. If you buy three books at £1.75 each, how much change will you get from £10?

3. What is 35×35 to the nearest 100?

4. A number is selected. Then 5 is subtracted and the answer multiplied by 7. The final answer is 35. What was the original number?

5. What is 2.5% of 500?

6. Find one-third of 20.1.

7. Write 17/100 as a decimal.

8. My house is 400 years old and my age is 3.5% of the age of my house. How old will I be in nine years time?

9. How long does it take to travel 210 miles at 35 mph?

10. In consecutive weeks attendances at a football ground are 34,800, 35,000 and 35,200. What was the average weekly attendance?

Calculator Practice

Calculator allowed – 5 minutes

1. 4.56 + 3.09
2. 0.98 × 34
3. What is 17% of 450?
4. 53.34 ÷ 21
5. Increase £367 by 5%.
6. Decrease $367 by 5%.
7. A fast-growing plant doubles its height every day. On Friday it is 24cm high. How high was it on Monday?
8. Add together 0.99, 9.09 and 99.9.
9. How long, in hours and minutes, will it take to travel 345 miles at 45 mph?
10. How many seconds are there in a day?

The Race

No calculator – 10 minutes

Here are the times taken by the runners in a race:
12m 34s, 11m 17s, 13m 45s, 11m 58s, 12m 02s,
14m 43s, 11m 09s, 14m 21s, 13m 15s, 14m 58s,
12m 45s, 14m 03s, 13m 57s

1. How many runners were there?
2. What is the difference in seconds between the fastest runner and the slowest?
3. What was the total time taken by the fastest three runners?
4. How many runners took less than 14 minutes?
5. What was the time taken by the runner who came sixth?
6. How many seconds did the winner take?
7. What was the total time in minutes, to the nearest minute, for all the runners?
8. How many runners were 30 seconds or less away from 13 minutes?
9. It was found that the time-keeper had been 15 seconds late in starting the stopwatch. How many runners had a time less than 14 minutes?
10. If the time-keeper had been 10 seconds early in starting the stopwatch, how many runners would have had a time less than 12 minutes?

Look for a Pattern

No calculator – 5 minutes

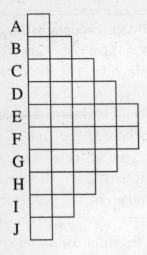

A. 25 less than B

B. $182 \div 7$

C. $14B + 9$

D. $13C - 24$

E. $13D - 3579$

F. $253 \times 254 - 67$

G. $13H + 295$

H. The number of days in a (non-leap) year + one and a half dozen

I. Twice the number of days in the fifth month

J. 50% of the difference between the squares of 1.5 and 0.5

Some Quick Percentages

Caculator allowed – 5 minutes

Populations:	Hilltown 32,506
	Larryville 28,432
	Pendennis 17,919

Give all the answers to the nearest whole number

1. What would the population of Hilltown be if it increased by 5%?
2. What would the population of Larryville be if it increased by 15%?
3. What would the population of Pendennis be if it increased by 20%?
4. What would the population of Hilltown be if it decreased by 5%?
5. What would the population of Larryville be if it decreased by 15%?
6. What would the population of Pendennis be if it decreased by 20%?
7. What is the percentage increase in the population of Hilltown if 550 new people come to live?
8. What is the percentage increase in the population of Larryville if 500 new people come to live?
9. What is the percentage increase in the population of Pendennis if 550 new people come to live?
10. What is the total population of all three towns if each increases its population by 7%?

Percentages

No calculator – 5 minutes

1. 5% of £200 is:
    a. £5   b. £10   c. £15   d. £20   e. £25

2. If 500 is decreased by 3% you get:
    a. 475   b. 485   c. 487   d. 495   e. 497

3. If 300 is increased by 7% you get:
    a. 307   b. 314   c. 321   d. 328   e. 335

4. A coat priced at $70 is reduced by 5%. The new price is:
    a. $63.50   b. $65   c. $66.50   d. $67.50   e. $68

5. An employee earning £12,000 receives a 10% pay rise. The new salary is:
    a. £12,120   b. £13,000   c. £13,120   d. £13,200
    e. £13,400

6. What is 8 as a percentage of 400
    a. 2   b. 4   c. 6   d. 8   e. 10

7. What is 8 as a percentage of 200
    a. 2   b. 4   c. 6   d. 8   e. 10

8. 3% of 3000 is:
    a. 30   b. 60   c. 90   d. 300   e. 600

9. 10% of 1 million is:
    a. 100   b. 1000   c. 100,000   d. 1,000,000
    e. none of these

10. 25% of one thousand is:
    a. 25   b. 125   c. 200   d. 250   e. 275

Number Pattern

No calculator – 5 minutes

Fill in the spaces with the answers indicated by the figures. All answers are single figures, and the sum of all the answers is 36.

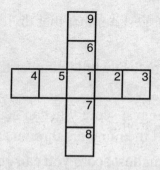

1. $(720 \times 3) - (30 \times 72)$
2. $29997 \div 9999$
3. $35552 \div 8888$
4. $38885 \div 7777$
5. $39996 \div 6666$
6. $(970 \times 25) - (194 \times 125) + 1$
7. $392 \div 56$
8. $3648 \div 456$
9. (1% of 5600) $\div 28$

Biggest and Smallest

Calculator allowed – 5 minutes

1. What is the biggest whole number with a square less than 7000?

2. What is the smallest whole number with a square greater than 700?

3. What is the biggest number that divides exactly into 12345?

4. What is the smallest whole number that will not divide exactly into 360?

5. What is the biggest score you can get throwing five dice, if all the numbers thrown are different?

6. What is the smallest score you can get throwing five dice, if all the numbers thrown are different?

7. What is the biggest total you can make if you use the digits 1, 2, 3, 4, 5, 6, 7, 8, 9 once each and make three, three-digit numbers that you add together?

8. What would be the smallest total you could get in question 7?

9. What is the biggest whole number with a square less than 700?

10. What is the smallest whole number with a square greater than 7000?

Ages

Calculator allowed – 5 minutes

Present Ages			
Men		Women	
Paul	31	Pam	27
Peter	35	Pat	32
Philip	47	Penelope	41

1. What will be the sum of all these ages in 17 years' time?

2. What was the sum of all these ages 19 years ago?

3. Multiply the age of the oldest man by that of the youngest woman.

4. Multiply the ages of the three men.

5. In 28 years' time, what will be the difference between the ages of the oldest woman and the youngest man?

6. What is the average age of the whole group?

7. When Pat's age has increased by 25%, how old will Philip be?

8. When Peter's age has increased by two-sevenths, how old will Pam be?

9. If Penelope was born in 1953, when will Peter be 52?

10. If Pam was born in 1967, when will Philip be 87?

Another Number Pattern

Calculator allowed – 5 minutes

Place the answers as indicated by the numbers and arrows.

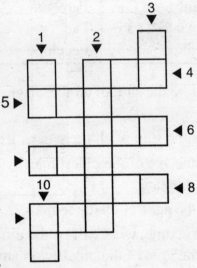

1. $432 \div 27$
2. 568×569
3. 8% of 700
4. $818.8 \div 2.3$
5. 100 less than twice the answer to question 4
6. $7 \times$ the answer to question 3
7. Square root of 12321
8. $1.5 \times$ the answer to question 5
9. 6 lots of 3 dozen + half a dozen
10. $2813 \div 97$

A Crossnumber

Calculator allowed – 10 minutes

1.		2.	3.	■	4.
	■	5.		6.	
7.	8.		■	9.	
10.		■	11.		
12.		13.		■	
	■	14.			

Across
1. 79×63
5. $20650 \div 7$
7. $19 \times (5$ across less 2900$)$
9. 5% of 1280
10. Divides exactly by 11
11. 11 down - 14
12. $101 \times 11 \times 9$
14. 107×30

Down
1. 1 less than 45% of a million
2. Number of seconds in 12 minutes
3. $4977 \div 63$
4. Number of seconds in a week
6. 9×63
8. 2 down - 121
11. 1/7th of 4900 less 8
13. 100 decreased by 7%

31

Travel

No calculator – 5 minutes

> I can: walk at 3 mph
>   jog at 5 mph
>   run at 6 mph
>   cycle at 10 mph
>   drive at 35 mph

How long will it take to:

1. Walk half a mile?
2. Drive 1000 miles?
3. Jog 62 miles?
4. Run 81 miles?
5. Cycle 500 miles?

How many miles can I:

6. Walk in 24 hours?
7. Jog in 48 hours?
8. Run in 72 hours?
9. Cycle in a day?
10. Drive in 120 hours?

Quick Sums

Calculator allowed – 5 minutes

1. 234×432
2. 541×145
3. 4.32×5.41
4. $5.41 \div 1.45$
5. 23.4% of 432
6. 54.1% of 145
7. $234432 - 145541$
8. $2.34 \times 1.45 \times 5.41$
9. $43.2 + 4.32 + 4.32$
10. 43.2% of 4.32% of 432

How Many?

Calculator allowed – 5 minutes

1. How many dozen in 1140?

2. How many inches in half a mile?

3. How many yards in 3 miles?

4. How many books costing $3.75 can I buy for $2100?

5. How many different arrangements are there of the letters P E T E ?

6. How many different arrangements are there of the letters F R E D ?

7. How many squares are there on half of a quarter of a chessboard?

8. How many people can travel on 371 coaches if there are 47 seats in each coach?

9. How many whole numbers divide exactly into 2431?

10. How many whole numbers have squares less than 1000?

Rows and Columns

No calculator – 5 minutes

1	2	3	4	5	6	7	8	9	10
11	12	13	14	15	16	17	18	19	20
21	22	23	24	25	26	27	28	29	30
31	32	33	34	35	36	37	38	39	40
41	42	43	44	45	46	47	48	49	50
51	52	53	54	55	56	57	58	59	60
61	62	63	64	65	66	67	68	69	70
71	72	73	74	75	76	77	78	79	80
81	82	83	84	85	86	87	88	89	90
91	92	93	94	95	96	97	98	99	100

1. What is the largest total for a row?
2. What is the largest total for a column?
3. What is the smallest total for a row?
4. What is the smallest total for a column?
5. What is the sum of all the rows?
6. What is the sum of all the columns?
7. What is the sum of all the numbers on the diagonal from 1 to 100?
8. What is the sum of all the numbers on the diagonal from 10 to 91?
9. What is the difference between the highest row total and the lowest column total?
10. What is the difference between the lowest row total and the highest column total?

More Mental Practice

No calculator – 15 minutes

1. 29 + 18
2. 15 - 7
3. 9 × 8
4. 54 ÷ 9
5. 55 + 32
6. 95 - 47
7. 12 × 23
8. 84 ÷ 3
9. 216 + 154
10. 328 - 256
11. 163 × 7
12. 364 ÷ 28

Add the columns:

13.	13	14.	325	15.	414	16.	258
	21		325		426		235
	28		325		416		267
	32		325		427		267
	16		325		439		264

17. Multiply 15 by 6 and add 12
18. Multiply 50 by 11 and subtract 7
19. Multiply 95 by 7 and add 53
20. Multiply 65 by 13 and subtract 11

Numbers and Measures

Calculator allowed – 20 minutes

Measures of length: 1cm = 10mm; 1m = 100cm
Measure of weight: 1 tonne = 1000kg

1. 1/2 + 3/4

2. 5.5 + 3.25

3. 600 × 3.25

4. 3.5 + 2.7

5. 3.05 + 4.4

6. 10% of 360

7. 25% of 440

8. 7% of 150

9. 6.25% of 220

10. 3 × 2.04

11. How many mm in 4cm?

12. How many mm in 12.66m?

13. How many mm in 21.08m?

14. How many kg in 2.3 tonnes?

15. How many kg in 3.08 tonnes?

16. A machine produces 600kg/hour. How many tonnes does it produce in a 12-hour shift?

17. A machine produces 600kg of pipe per hour. The pipe weighs 1.4kg per metre. How many metres of pipe, to the nearest 10 metres, are produced per hour?

18. In a shift a machine uses 41 tonnes of material. 5.25 tonnes are wasted as scrap. What is the percentage of material wasted to the nearest one-tenth of a per cent?

19. A worker works a 52-week year, 38 hours a week, for an annual salary of £7113.60.
   a. What is the salary per week?
   b. What is the salary per hour?
   c. What would the worker get for 8 hours at time-and-a-half?
   d. If a 6.25% increase in salaries is agreed, find the new annual salary and the new rate per week.

World Time Differences

Calculator allowed – 10 minutes

Time differences from London (in hours) are:

Beijing	+8
Kuwait	+3
Paris	+1
London	0
New York	-5
Los Angeles	-8
Honolulu	-10

1. A traveller leaves Beijing at 1300 on 5 April and, after 15 hours travelling westwards, arrives in New York. What is the local time and date on arrival?
2. A flight from Honolulu to Paris, travelling east, leaves at 1415 on 7 March and, after delays, takes 21 hours to reach Paris. What is the local time and date on arrival?
3. It is 1732 in London. What time will it be 15 minutes later in Los Angeles?
4. A flight leaves New York for London at 1325. The flying time is 7½ hours. A passenger has a watch that is correct on departure but that loses 2 minutes every hour. The passenger also puts his watch on by 70 minutes just before landing. What time will the watch show on landing?

5. Three friends in Kuwait, Beijing and New York book a simultaneous telephone conversation for 0935 London time. If the call lasts 12 minutes, what will be the local times in Kuwait and New York when it finishes?

6. It is 2358 in New York on 13 May. What is the date and time in Beijing?

7. It is 0640 in Honolulu on 28 February 1995. What is the date and time in Kuwait?

8. A traveller leaves London at 0730 on a 6-hour flight to New York, spends 7 hours in New York and then flies back to London on a flight taking 5½ hours. What is the time of arrival back in London?

9. What is the time in Los Angeles when it is 0017 in Beijing?

10. What is the time in Beijing when it is 0017 in Los Angeles?

International Air Distances

Calculator allowed – 10 minutes

	London	Moscow	New York	Rome
London	–	1556	3473	892
Moscow		–	4680	1477
New York			–	4293
Rome				–

All distances are in miles

1. How far is it from New York to Moscow via Rome?
2. If you start in Rome and fly to the other three capitals and back to Rome, what is the smallest total number of miles you will have done?
3. A passenger travels from London to New York and back every week for a year. How far will she have travelled in the year?
4. A plane has to be serviced after 50,000 miles flying. It has done six return trips between Rome and Moscow already. How many more return trips can it do before a service is needed (it must not exceed 50,000 miles before the service)?
5. A salesman has to travel from London to each of the other capitals and back once every month. How many miles will he travel in a year?

6. Fares are calculated at $0.15 per mile What is the cost of:
a. a return fare from London to Rome?
b. a single fare from Moscow to New York?
c. a return fare from Rome to London via Moscow?

7. How many single trips between London and New York will be needed in order to travel one million miles?

8. A flight from Moscow to New York is forced to make a diversion which increases the distance by 7 per cent What is the distance travelled?

9. An airline charges 7.6 pence per mile. What is the cost of a return ticket from London to Rome to the nearest 10 pence.

10. A ticket from New York to Moscow and back costs $3931.20. What is the cost per mile?

International Paper Sizes

Calculator allowed – 10 minutes

A0	1189x841
A1	841x594
A2	594x420
A3	420x297
A4	297x210
A5	210x148
A6	148x105
A7	105x74

All measurements are in mm, 1 inch = 25.4 mm

1. To the nearest inch
a. What is the length in inches of A3?
b. What is the length in inches of A0?
c. What is the width in inches of A2?
d. What is the width in inches of A7?

2. How many sheets of A7 are needed to cover the same area as one sheet of A0?

3. A poster, which was A4 size, is changed to A1 size. What is the percentage increase in area?

4. What is the difference in total area between 5 sheets of A2 and 12 sheets of A6?

5. What is the difference in length between 150 sheets of A2 and 45 sheets of A0?

6. If paper costs 0.0003p per square cm, what will 500 sheets of A4 cost to the nearest pence?

7. For $1.00 you can buy 1000 sheets of A1 or 350 sheets of A4. Which is the better buy in terms of area of paper bought?

8. How many sheets of A6 would be needed to cover a rectangular table top measuring 3 feet by 5 feet?

9. If 100 sheets of paper (any size) are 0.75 inches thick, what is the difference in volume (in cubic centimetres) between 1000 sheets of A1 and 100 sheets of A5?

10. What is the difference in area in mm^2 between 1 million sheets of A1 and 1 million sheets of A7?

House Numbers

No calculator – 10 minutes

Mr and Mrs Rule live in a road in which there are 200
houses. The odd-numbered houses are on the south
side, and the even-numbered ones are on the north
side – for example, house No 1 is exactly opposite
No. 2, No. 3 is opposite No. 4 and so on.

1. What is the sum of the numbers of the last four
   houses on the north side?
2. What is the sum of the first ten houses on the
   south side?

3. Mr and Mrs Rule live on the opposite side of the road from Mr and Mrs Darby.
'My number is 21 more than yours,' said Mrs Rule to Mrs Darby.
'And if you multiply 15 by itself you get the sum of both our numbers,' said Mrs Darby.
What are the two numbers?

4. How many numbers in the road have two digits and end in 9?

5. The house doors are all exactly 10 metres apart and it is 15 metres across the road from one front door to another. A postman walks to every front door in the order 1, 2, 4, 3, 5, 6, 8, 7 and so on. How far has he walked by the time he reaches No. 15?

6. How far would the postman walk if he visited all the odd numbers first and then all the even numbers, starting at No. 1 and finishing at No. 2?

7. The local council is ordering new numbers to put on the doors. How many individual digits are needed for the whole road?

8. What is the sum of the numbers on the south side from 17 to 27 inclusive?

9. What is the sum of the numbers on the north side from 18 to 28 inclusive?

10. All the houses have the same number of bricks. There are 5,912,600 bricks in the whole road. How many bricks are there in each house?

Getting Harder?

Calculator allowed – 15 minutes

1. What is the largest whole number that, when multiplied by itself, is less than 5000?

2. Tom has his hair cut every 35 days, Basil every 42 days. They both had their hair cut on 1 January 1995. When will they next have their hair cut on the same day?

3. A clock takes 4 seconds to strike 5 o'clock. How long will it take to strike 8 o'clock

4. In a shooting competition 5 points are scored for a 'bull', 3 for an 'inner', 1 for an 'outer' and 0 for a miss. In how many ways can you score 13 points in 5 shots?

5. The combined ages of a family of five total 96. What did the combined ages total 7 years ago, if the youngest member of the family is now 7?

6. Thirty-two teams enter a knock-out competition. How many matches will there be in the whole competition if there are no draws?

7. Find three consecutive numbers whose product is 140556.

8. Find three consecutive numbers whose sum is 342.

9. Every hour a cyclist rides 15 miles and then takes a 10 minute rest. How long will the cyclist take to travel 70 miles?

10. In an election 1000 votes were cast for the three candidates, X, Y and Z.
    X beat Y by 35 votes.
    Z obtained 50% of the vote achieved by Y.
    How many votes did X get?

Spring Folly?

No calculator – 5 minutes

In this test, if you substitute a letter for each answer, using A=1, B=2, etc., you should spell out two words.

1. One less than the number of prime numbers between 20 and 30

2. Decrease 20 by 20%

3. Half of three dozen

4. The smallest square number that divides by 3

5. Number of hours in one-fourteenth of a week

6. Nine less than the sum of the digits of the number of days in a leap year

7. $0.1 \times 0.2 \times 0.3 \times 2500$

8. $1 \times 2 \times 3 \times 2.5$

9. $G + O + T - I - J - K$

The Meeting

No calculator – 10 minutes

Mr Chapman, Miss Rogers, Mrs Pocock and Mr Taylor need to arrange a meeting.

It is now Friday, 20 May. Monday, 30 May is a public holiday.

Mr Chapman cannot manage Tuesday or Thursday mornings, and he is on holiday for a week beginning 6 June.

Miss Rogers is away for four days starting on 14 June.

Mrs Pocock can never be available on Mondays, Wednesdays or Thursdays.

Mr Taylor is unavailable on alternate Fridays starting on Friday, 27 May.

A meeting cannot be held on a Saturday, Sunday or public holiday.

1. On how many mornings between 23 May and 17 June inclusive could all four people attend a meeting?
2. How many complete days are available for a meeting between 23 May and 17 June inclusive?
3. On how many days between 23 May and 17 June inclusive, excluding Saturdays, Sundays and the public holiday, are all four people unable to attend a meeting for all or part of the day?
4. If a meeting lasting two days is needed, what are the first possible dates assuming that a Saturday could be used as one of the days?
5. Mrs Pocock has to be at the meeting together with any two of the others. What is the first possible day for a meeting?
6. If any three people have to attend and the fourth person does not matter, what is the earliest possible day for a meeting?
7. For how many half days is Mr Chapman available in the period 23 May to 17 June inclusive, excluding Saturdays, Sundays and the public holiday?
8. For how many whole days is Miss Rogers available in the period 23 May to 17 June inclusive, excluding Saturdays, Sundays and the public holiday?
9. In the period 23 May to 27 May inclusive, for what percentage of half days is Mr Chapman available?
10. What is the first Friday in July on which Mr Taylor will be available?

Numbers

No calculator – 10 minutes

1. 719 × 23 is equal to:
   a. 16432   b. 16435   c. 16535   d. 16537   e. 16539

2. 17.5% of £500 is
   a. £8.75   b. £18.75   c. £87.50   d. £87.75   e. £187.50

3. 0.35 × 0.2 is equal to:
   a. 0.0007   b. 0.007   c. 0.07   d. 0.7   e. none of these

4. 60 as a percentage of 360 is:
   a. just under 16.6   b. just over 16.6   c. less than 16
   d. more than 17   e. none of these

5. The sum of the first 7 odd numbers (starting at 1) is:
   a. 19   b. 29   c. 39   d. 49   e. 64

6. One million dollars is shared equally among eight
   people. Each gets:
   a. $12,500   b. $62,500   c. $1250   d. $6250
   e. $125,000

7. The smallest number that, when multiplied by
   itself, is more than 9000 is:
   a. 91   b. 92   c. 93   d. 94   e. 95

8. 63 people are all the same age. Half the sum of
   their ages is 945. Each person is aged:
   a. 15   b. 20   c. 25   d. 30   e. 35

9. A TV programme lasts 135 minutes. It finishes at 23.56. It started at:

    a. 20.41   b. 20.51   c. 21.41   d. 21.51   e. after 21.00

10. 5% of 10% of 200 is:

    a. 1   b. 5   c. 10   d. 15   e. 25

Q28   **A18**

More Numbers

Calculator allowed – 10 minutes

1. 63% of 0.988 is:
   a. 0.043344   b. 0.6174   c. 0.62240   d. 0.62244
   e. 0.64244

2. (2.3 - 0.8)/(2.3 + 0.7) is equal to:
   a. 0.325   b. 0.4   c. 0.425   d. 0.5   e. 0.525

3. I have three-sevenths of a journey to complete. If I have travelled 108 miles so far, the total length of the journey is:
   a. 189 miles   b. 198 miles   c. 225 miles
   d. 252 miles   e. none of these

4. A speed of 50ft per second is about the same as:
   a. 14 mph   b. 24 mph   c. 34 mph   d. 44 mph
   e. 54 mph

5. As a percentage of 500, 0.1 is:
   a. 0.002%   b. 0.02%   c. 0.2%   d. 2%   e. 20%

---

6. If a sheet of paper measures 7 × 4.3in, 63 identical sheets will have a total area of about:
   a. 130 sq in   b. 130 sq ft   c. 13 sq in   d. 13 sq ft
   e. 1300 sq in

7. The number of seconds in two weeks is:
   a. 10,080   b. 20,160   c. 1,209,600   d. 1,512,000
   e. 3,024,000

8. $4000 earns interest at 6.5% per annum. After one year it will have earned:
   a. $26   b. $260   c. $2600   d. $280
   e. none of these

9. If you write down all the numbers from 1 to 40 inclusive, the digit '1' is used:
   a. 10 times   b. 11 times   c. 12 times   d. 13 times
   e. 14 times

10. 0.3% of 0.7% of 0.1 is equal to:
    a. 0.0000007   b. 0.000007   c. 0.0007   d. 0.007
    e. none of these

Look for Symmetry!

Calculator allowed – 10 minutes

1.		2.	3.		4.
	■	5.		■	
6.	7.			8.	
9.					
	■	10.		■	
11.					

Across

1. 25% of 999900
5. 8/5ths of 10 across
6. (70707 × 11) - 300003
9. 55 × 10667
10. 5/8ths of 5 across
11. 72227 × 11

Down

1. (5864 × 40) +7
2. 164609 × 6
3. ((405 × 405) + 584) × 0.6/0.1
4. $731^2 + 14^2 + 10$
7. 999922 less than 1 million
8. 99922 less than one hundred thousand

Telephones

Calculator allowed – 15 minutes

Mobile Telephone Tariffs

	Scheme A	Scheme B	Scheme C
Connection	£29.50	£29.50	£29.50
Monthly line rental	£11.99	£13.99	£17.99
Call charges: off-peak	£0.65	£0.20	£0.34
peak	£0.65	£0.50	£0.34

Call charges are for each minute or part of a minute

1. If no calls are made, what is the difference in cost between the cheapest and most expensive scheme over a year?

2. What does scheme B cost altogether (including connection) over 3 months if 13.5 minutes of peak calls and 143.6 minutes of off-peak calls are made?

3. How many minutes of calls are needed to make scheme C cheaper than scheme A?

4. Calls totalling 360 minutes are made in one month. What is the difference in cost between scheme A and scheme C?

5. All the prices given include tax at 17.5%. If the tax is increased to 20%, what will be the new connection charge to the nearest pence?

6. An organization has one phone under scheme A, two phones under scheme B and three phones under scheme C. What is the total rental bill for a year?

7. If you make 100 minutes of peak calls and 50 minutes of off-peak calls in a month, which is the best scheme to use and how much cheaper is it than the second best?

8. A special offer for scheme B allows free connection and all calls at half price for a month. What is the total saving if 55 minutes of peak calls and 65 minutes of off-peak calls are made?

9. All charges are increased by 7%. What is the new line rental per month for scheme C to the nearest pence?

10. You expect to make no peak calls and 500 minutes of off-peak calls in a year. What is the total cost of the cheapest scheme?

A Pack of Cards

No calculator – 10 minutes

A pack of cards consists of 52 cards numbered A, 2, 3, 4, 5, 6, 7, 8, 9, 10, J, Q, K in the four suits, clubs, diamonds, hearts and spades.

1. What is the sum of all the numbers on the cards in a pack?

2. What percentage of cards have letters on them?

3. If A, J, Q and K were replaced by 1, 11, 12 and 13, what would be the sum of all the numbers on the cards in the pack?

4. What percentage of the cards are red and have odd numbers on them?

5. What percentage of the cards are red with no numbers on them?

6. What percentage of the cards are black queens or black kings?

7. What answer do you get if you multiply together all the even numbers on the spades in the pack?

8. What answer do you get if you multiply together all the odd numbers on the clubs in the pack?

9. If you pick up 10 cards with numbers on them, what are the highest and lowest totals you could have?

10. If each card measures 3×4cm, what is the total area that could be covered using all the cards?

A Message from 5600

Calculator allowed – 10 minutes

Answer the questions. Put the letters against the appropriate answers in the list and, reading downwards, you will spell out a message.

A Decrease 5600 by 6%
E Increase 5600 by 12%
G Increase 5600 by 5%
H 5% of 5600
I 15% of 5600
O Increase 5600 by 15%
O Decrease 5600 by 15%
T 6% of 5600
T Decrease 5600 by 12%
U 12% of 5600
V Decrease 5600 by 5%
Y Increase 5600 by 6%

Answer	Letter
_9_6	
4__0	
_72	
_8_	
5__4	
5_2_	
6__2	
_88_	
_44_	
3__	
_4_	
4__8	

Four Numbers

Calculator allowed – 10 minutes

All the questions are about the four numbers 36, 72, 144 and 288.

1. Write down all the possible products of pairs of these numbers (six answers).

2. Add together all the answers in question 1.

3. Write down the squares of the four numbers (four answers).

4. Add together the answers in question 3.

5. What is the first number as a percentage of the last?

6. Increase each number by 1/18th and find the sum of the four new numbers.

7. Decrease each number by one-ninth and find the sum of the four new numbers.

8. How many dozen in the sum of the four numbers?

9. If the four numbers represent numbers of minutes, how many hours are there in their total?

10. If the four numbers represent days, how many complete weeks are there in their total?

A Stay in a Hotel

Calculator allowed – 10 minutes

Accommodation and breakfast

Single room with shower   £39.50 per person
Double room with shower   £35.40 per person
Double room with bath   £37.40 per person

Dinner   £17.50 per person

*Children under 14 pay half the dinner rate
but full room rates*

Special two-day break

**Two nights' accommodation,
breakfast and dinner:**

Single room with shower   £92.00 per person
Double room with shower   £82.00 per person
Double room with bath   £84.50 per person

Children under 14: 5% off these rates

1. Three couples each book a double room with bath for one night and all have dinner. What is the total bill?
2. For one couple, what is the saving on a double room with shower and dinner if the Special Break is taken rather than paying normal rates for two nights?
3. A family of two adults and three children, aged

15, 13 and 11, spend seven nights at the hotel, eating dinner each night. The adults occupy a double room with shower, and the children each have a single room. All have dinner each night. What is the total bill?

4. What is the percentage saving for a single room with dinner for two nights if the Special Break is taken rather than normal rates being paid?

5. What is the percentage saving for a double room with bath and dinner for two nights if the Special Break is taken rather than normal rates being paid?

6. The hotel has 7 single rooms, 17 double rooms with shower and 12 double rooms with bath. It is full with adults for one night and all guests have dinner. What is the total income for the night?

7. Two American couples occupy two double rooms with bath and they all have dinner. They wish to pay in American dollars. What must they pay if the exchange rate offered is £1 for $1.55?

8. A group consisting of three couples and five single people wish to book for five nights with dinner. The double rooms all have a shower. A 15% discount is agreed for the group. What is the total bill?

9. A couple with a 7-year-old child take a Special Break. What is the total cost if the couple have a room with bath and the child a single room?

10. The hotel opens a block of seven additional single rooms with shower. What extra income would these rooms produce if they were all occupied for 312 nights in a year?

Train Times

Calculator allowed – 15 minutes

1. What is the quickest possible journey time, in hours and minutes, from Kingsville to Dupyville on a Saturday?

2. How many minutes does it take to get from Kingsville to Dankworth on the train leaving Kingsville at 0930 on a Friday?

3. How long does the slowest possible train take from Dupyville to Kingsville on a Sunday?

4. A traveller catches the 0818 train from Dankworth to Kingsville and returns on the 1730 train from Kingsville to Dankworth every Monday for 6 weeks. What is the total time spent on the train in the 6 weeks, assuming that all trains run on time?

Mondays to Fridays / Saturdays / Sundays

Mondays to Fridays			Saturdays			Sundays		
KINGSVILLE depart	DANKWORTH arrive	DUPYVILLE arrive	KINGSVILLE depart	DANKWORTH arrive	DUPYVILLE arrive	KINGSVILLE depart	DANKWORTH arrive	DUPYVILLE arrive
0600	0858	0916	0600	0857	0915	0900	1227	1246
0730	0957	1014	0700	0938	0956	1000	1318	—
A 0800	1022	1051	0800	1033	1052	1025	1348	1406
0900	1123	1157	0830	1058	—	1100	1418	1437
B 1000	1239	1257	0900	1133	1200	1200	1513	1532
1100	1317	—	0930	1208	1226	1225	1547	—
1100	1329	—	B 1000	1234	—	1300	1613	1632
1130	1404	1421	1040	1311	1329	1325	1638	1705
1230	1504	1521	1100	1329	—	1400	1713	1732
1300	1517	1543	1130	1408	1426	1500	1813	1855
1330	1604	1621	1200	1442	1501	1525	1847	1905
1400	1621		1230	1503	1521	1600	1910	1949
1430	1659	1716	1300	1529	1600	1700	1948	2007
A 1500	1736	1757	1330	1603	1621	1730	2032	2051
1530	1804	1821	1400	1631	—	1800	2051	2125
1600	1820	1858	1500	1728	1746	1900	2147	2206
1630	1906	1923	1600	1835	1857	2000	2247	2306
1700	1917	1951	1700	1928	1946	2100	2355	0014
C 1730	1953	2010	1800	2036	2054	2200	0100	0119
1800	2025	2059	1900	2145	2203			
1830	2111	2128	2030	2306	2324			
1900	2133	2150						
2000	2232	2252						
2200	0047	0106						

A the Dankworth Express
B the Dupyville Express
C the Kingsville Pullman

Times in **bold** indicate a direct service.
Times in light indicate a connecting service.

Mondays to Fridays / Saturdays / Sundays

Mondays to Fridays			Saturdays			Sundays		
DUPYVILLE depart	DANKWORTH depart	KINGSVILLE arrive	DUPYVILLE depart	DANKWORTH depart	KINGSVILLE arrive	DUPYVILLE depart	DANKWORTH depart	KINGSVILLE arrive
A 0612	0630	0900	0017	0035	0500	0743	0801	1133
B 0642	0700	0935	0613	0631	0909	0842	0900	1243
A 0712	0730	0952	0713	0731	1011	—	0956	1333
—	0737	1014	0743	0801	1045	1058	1116	1453
0757	0818	1107	0812	0830	1112	—	1215	1539
0842	0900	1145	0854	0912	1151	1258	1316	1635
0912	0930	1218	0913	0931	1224	1317	1356	1711
0923	1004	1239	0923	1001	1244	1351	1420	1725
1043	1101	1339	0959	1029	1307	1417	1446	1748
—	1141	1418	1044	1102	1344	1501	1519	1831
1118	1201	1440	1106	1124	1408	1515	1541	1836
1243	1301	1545	1118	1201	1441	1546	1604	1907
1342	1400	1649	1244	1302	1543	1559	1626	1924
—	1457	1739	1343	1401	1651	—	1700	2003
1538	1556	1847	—	1428	1716	1713	1731	2039
—	1616	1855	1514	1532	1813	1753	1811	2118
1647	1705	1958	1527	1631	1923	1846	1904	2208
1728	1756	2040	1711	1729	2021	1949	2007	2330
1853	1911	2157	1817	1834	2125			
—	1931	2229	—	1857	2140			
2048	2106	0008	1922	1940	2226			

Times in **bold** indicate a direct service.
Times in light indicate a connecting service.

A the Dupyville Pullman
B the Kingsville Pullman

5. A passenger has a watch that gains 3 minutes every hour, The watch is correct as the passenger gets on the 1243 train from Dupyville to Kingsville on a Tuesday. What time (to the nearest minute) will the watch show when the train reaches Kingsville, assuming the train is on time?

6. A train reaches Dankworth from Kingsville at 1913 on a Sunday. It is running 26 minutes late. At what time did it leave Kingsville?

7. Which is faster on a journey from Kingsville to Dankworth, the Monday Kingsville Pullman or the Saturday Dupyville Express and by how many minutes?

8. What is the difference in minutes between the fastest train from Dupyville to Kingsville on a Saturday and the fastest train between the same places on a Sunday

9. If all the journey times are increased by 10% because of track repairs, what is now the shortest time, in minutes, from Dupyville to Dankworth on a Sunday?

10. A passenger leaves Kingsville on the 0600 train on a Tuesday, travels to Dupyville, gets the next possible train back to Kingsville and then the next possible train back to Dupyville. At what time will the passenger finally arrive in Dupyville and how many minutes will have been spent travelling?

Numbers in a Day

No calculator – 10 minutes

1. I get up at 0716 and go to bed at 2323. For how many minutes have I been up?
2. I have 7 tins of tea bags left. Each tin contains 56 bags. I use 9 bags each day. How many days will my supply last?
3. My watch gains 0.5 minutes every hour. I put it right at 0720. What time will it say when the real time is 2320
4. I spend 35 minutes travelling to work and 55 minutes travelling home. What percentage of the day is taken up by this travelling?
5. I spend 3 minutes each day watching the weather forecast on TV. How many hours, to the nearest hour, is this in a non-leap year?
6. My heating bill for a year is £567. How much is this per week on average to the nearest pence?
7. I spend 27% of my time asleep. How many hours, to the nearest hour, is this in May?
8. Every week I use 30 litres of fuel at 65p per litre. What do I spend on fuel in a year?
9. My staircase has 15 steps. I go up and down 19 times a day. How many steps have I been up in a day?
10. My house has twice as many windows as my neighbour's house. The two houses have four dozen windows together. How many windows does my house have?

Numbers Everywhere

Calculator allowed – 10 minutes

Library opening hours

Mon-Fri	9.30 am	–	12.30 pm
	2.00 pm	–	5.00 pm
Sat	9.30 am	–	12.00

Hire Charges

All items cost $5.50 + amount shown
+ sales tax at 17.5%

Ladder	$3.00 per day
Chain saw	$7.00 per day
Carpet cleaner	$5.60 per day
Scaffolding	$15.80 per day

Cheese prices

Cheddar	£3.10 per lb
Stilton	£4.24 per lb
Brie	£2.95 per lb
Roquefort	£2.87 per lb

SALE!!!!!
15% off all prices below

Suits	£112
Jackets	£85
Trousers	£36
Shirts	£24

1. For how many hours is the library open in a 15-week period?

2. What is the cost of 2½lb of Cheddar together with ¾lb of Stilton?

3. What is the cost of hiring a carpet cleaner for three days to the nearest dollar?

4. What will a suit and shirt cost together?

5. The library decides to close all day on Thursdays. What is the percentage reduction in opening hours?

6. A dealer buys 50lb of each cheese. What is the total cost if a 20% discount is allowed?

7. Scaffolding is hired for 17 days. What is the cost to the nearest dollar?

8. What would 17 jackets have cost originally?

9. How many whole pounds of Roquefort cheese could be bought for £336?

10. What percentage of library opening time is before noon?

Windows, Golf Balls, CDs and Bestwood House

Calculator allowed – 15 minutes

BESTWOOD HOUSE

Bestwood House will be open every day from Saturday, 7 August, until 1 October. Opening hours are from 9.30 am to 5.30 pm and the last admission is at 4.30 pm.

The picture gallery is open from 10.00 am to 5.00 pm on Tuesdays to Saturdays and from 2.00 to 5.00 pm on Sundays.

The gardens are open on Tuesdays, Wednesdays and Thursdays until 30 September and on Wednesdays only from 6 October to 22 December. Opening hours are from noon until 4.00 pm.

WINDOWS

5 windows any size $1600
6 windows any size $1700
7 windows any size $1800
8 windows any size $1900
9 windows any size $2000

or special 'Monarch' windows (any size) $170 each

Golf Balls

Buy 20 balls and get 15 free!
35 balls for just £22 plus £3.75 P&

Buy 40 balls get 40 free!
80 balls for just $42 plus £3.75 P&

20th Century Classics

Lyle Lovett CD at £8.99 (RRP £9.99)

Battleship Potemkin at £13.99 (RRP 14.99)

Catch 22 at £5.99

1. What is the cost per window if you buy eight windows?

2. How many hours is Bestwood House open in a full week?

3. How many hours is the picture gallery open altogether from 7 August until 15 August inclusive?

4. How many *Battleship Potemkin* CDs can be bought for £150?

5. If you buy 40 balls and get 40 free, what is the cost per ball, including postage and packing, to the nearest pence?

6. For how many days is Bestwood House open altogether?

7. *Lyle Lovett* CD is reduced by 15%. What is the new price to the nearest pence?

8. You want to receive exactly 400 golf balls. What is your total bill, including postage and packing.

9. If you buy nine 'Monarch' windows what is the percentage reduction on the normal price?

10. For what total number of days will the gardens be open in October, November and December?

Taxing Problems

Calculator allowed – 10 minutes

On money earned in a year tax has to be paid as follows:

The first £3750 is free of tax
Tax is paid at 20% on the next £2500
Tax is paid at 25% on the next £17,500
Tax is paid at 40% on any additional income

Find the annual tax bill for the following incomes:

1. £5000

2. £10,000

3. £15,000

4. £20,000

5. £25,000

6. £1,000,000

7. £37,400

8. £100,000

9. £3950

10. £395,000

Shares, Savings, Daylight & Walking

Calculator allowed – 15 minutes

Savers' Selection

	Minimum Deposit	Rate per Annum
Coobah Bank	$100	5.84%
Drayton Investments	$500	6.75%
Eiger Ltd	$10,000	7.05%
Fourways Bank	$25,000	7.25%
Gloomish Inc.	$500	6.50%
Harvester Bank	$10,500	7.35%

Daylight today

	Sunrise	Sunset	Moonrise	Moonset
Jayton	05:56	20:33	02:55	18:51
Kupton	06:04	20:52	03:02	19:12
Litton	05:50	20:56	02:43	19:17
Maton	05:40	20:30	02:35	18:49
Niton	05:44	20:49	02:36	19:11
Orton	05:52	20:40	02:48	18:59
Picton	05:44	20:21	02:43	18:38

Women's 10km Walk, Final
The times of the contestants were:

1. 42 m 59s
2. 43.08
3. 43.21
4. 43.26
5. 43.28
6. 43.33
7. 43.47
8. 43.56
9. 44.13
10. 44.17
11. 45.06
12. 45.17
13. 45.24
14. 45.57
15. 46.11
16. 46.13
17. 46.22
18. 46.31
19. 46.41
20. 46.45
21. 46.48
22. 46.58
23. 47.03
24. 47.20
25. 47.24
26. 47.41
27. 47.45
28. 47.5l
29. 47.54
30. 47.56
31. 48.03
32. 48.08
33. 48.23
34. 48.24
35. 48.36
36. 48.39
37. 48.43
38. 49.06
39. 49.08
40. 49.18
41. 49.24
42. 50.22

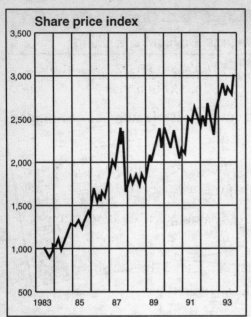

Share price index

XYZ
Share price

Main changes this week

Up	week's change %	close
Alpha Ltd	14.0	650
Theta Group	12.7	133
Rialto Inc	10.2	162
Sigma Corp	9.4	967
Beta Ltd	8.0	332.5
Down	week's change %	close
BBB Group	-9.4	634
Backup Inc	-6.8	413
Astra Ltd	-6.5	6125
Tonkers	-6.2	226
Stoomey Ltd	-5.3	162

1. What was the price of Theta Group shares last week?

2. What interest will you get on an account in the Fourways Bank for $26,000 in a year?

3. What is the maximum possible number of minutes of sunshine in Picton

4. By what percentage (approximately) did XYZ shares increase from December to June?

5. What was the average time for the first four women?

6. By roughly what percentage did the share price index increase during 1984?

7. What was the price of Tonkers shares last week?

8. What was the highest value (nearest 100) of the share price index between 1983 and 1988?

9. By how many seconds did the woman in 3rd place beat the woman in 37th place?

10. How much interest will $2500 in a Gloomish Inc account earn in a year?

Hotels

Calculator allowed – 10 minutes

Holidays in Esparto

		FINGAL				IRIS				MINTO		
Nights	7	10	11	14	7	10	11	14	7	10	11	14
1 May – 7 May	779	994	1062	1329	406	478	510	604	392	470	501	586
8 May – 14 May	784	996	1064	1331	408	480	512	606	403	473	504	597
15 May – 20 May	787	998	1066	1333	417	483	513	610	413	493	524	613
21 May – 25 May	791	1006	1144	1409	446	515	547	653	428	516	547	649
26 May – 11 June	931	1233	1336	1647	468	563	595	690	477	569	600	704
12 June – 25 June	960	1274	1382	1692	478	582	613	716	482	579	610	715
26 June – 9 July	965	1275	1383	1692	477	584	616	721	498	613	644	736
10 July – 16 July	975	1308	1384	1698	482	587	619	722	502	615	646	747
17 July – 30 July	983	1299	1407	1708	486	599	632	730	503	612	643	752
31 July – 20 Aug	982	1304	1402	1691	501	603	635	740	509	625	656	755
21 Aug – 3 Sep	980	1289	1397	1688	497	596	628	727	503	612	643	745
4 Sep – 10 Sep	972	1273	1381	1683	488	588	620	713	495	609	640	739
11 Sep – 17 Sep	961	1273	1381	1667	486	579	611	699	493	578	619	717
18 Sep – 1 Oct	907	1143	1251	1479	448	542	574	658	471	541	572	670
2 Oct – 15 Oct	789	1004	1072	1319	433	513	545	621	437	513	559	630
16 Oct – 24 Oct	764	999	1067	1314	427	496	545	591	432	496	549	600

Departures on or between

Prices shown are in £s per person

1. What is the total cost of the cheapest holiday for four people for 14 nights?

2. A party of 10 wishes to stay at the hotel Minto for 10 nights departing on the 1 July. The travel agent agrees to a 5% discount. What is the total cost for the party?

3. What is the total cost of the most expensive holiday for two people for seven nights?

4. If there are two daily flights from 1 May to 24 October inclusive, how many flights will there be altogether during this period?

5. What is the difference in £ between the cheapest and most expensive holidays for 11 nights?

6. If all departures after 1 October are reduced by 10%, how much will it cost for a party of six to depart on 14 October and stay at the Iris for 10 nights?

7. Two people wish to go to Esparto for seven nights but do not want to spend more than £450 each. On how many weeks is this possible at the hotel Minto?

8. What is the difference between the cheapest and most expensive holiday for a party of eight for 14 nights departing on 15 July?

9. Answer question 8, but with departure on 5 September

10. If you add the numbers in each row in the table, which row has the lowest total and what is it?

More Mental Practice

No calculator – 10 minutes

1. Find 7.5% of 1700
2. Find $14 \times 15 \times 16$
3. Add together the numbers of the years from 1996 to 2000 inclusive
4. Find 0.07×0.007
5. My father was born in 1950. In the year 2000 I shall be twice the age he was in 1963. How old will I be in 2015?
6. In a farm with 19 sheep, 23 chickens and 42 rabbits, how many legs do all the animals together have?
7. Add together 12.63, 12.67, 13.19 and 13.81
8. 23,500 people watch a game. If the game lasts 1.5 hours, how many 'person hours' have been spent watching?
9. A product costs 43p per litre or part of a litre. What will 20.78 litres cost?
10. What is the smallest number that will divide by both 91 and 11?

More Calculator Practice

Calculator allowed – 10 minutes

1. Find 76.9×67.8
2. Calculate $0.123 \times 5.789 \div 0.34$
3. How many minutes are there in 73 days?
4. How many boxes at \$1.45 a box can I buy for \$2900?
5. What is 1/15th of 75,000?
6. Calculate: $\dfrac{0.76 \div 0.54}{0.54 \div 0.76}$
7. Calculate: $\dfrac{0.76 \div 5.4}{7.6 \div 54}$
8. What is the average of 5.67, 4.56, 9.23 and 7.65?
9. My birthday is 73 days after 10 August and my brother's birthday is 18 days before mine. What is the date of my brother's birthday?
10. Express 567 as a percentage of 567,567

Train Fares

No calculator – 5 minutes

These are the fares between six towns

From/to	A	B	C	D	E	F
A	–	17	29	31	33	35
B		–	14	26	38	42
C			–	51	53	67
D				–	76	88
E					–	113

All amounts are in $

Calculate the fares for the following journeys:

1. A to C via B
2. F to D via E
3. C to B via D
4. B to A via F
5. F to B via E
6. B to C via F
7. A to E via D
8. A to F via E
9. C to F via A
10. A journey starting at A and visiting F, B, D, C, E in that order before returning to A

Palindromic Number

Calculator allowed – 10 minutes

Palindromic words are those that read the same both backwards and forwards – for example, anna, rotor and pip – and a well-known palindromic sentence is: 'Madam I'm Adam.'

Similarly, palindromic numbers read the same both ways – for example, 12521, 353 and 9876789.

1. Find 12521×11

2. Add together all the palindromic year numbers for years in the 20th and 21st centuries.

3. Add together all the palindromic numbers that lie between 10 and 100

4. Find $44444444 \div 11$

5. Find 987.789×123.321

6. Find $(809 \times 809) - 25$

7. Find $(908 \times 908) - 40$

8. Find $(11 \times 22 \times 33 \times 44 \times 55) - 3729$

9. Find 1122211×11

10. Add together 12344321, 32100123, 12355321 and 43100134.

Number Miscellany

Calculator allowed – 10 minutes

1. Add together all the dates in March.
2. Add together the squares of the numbers from 1 to 12 inclusive.

3. If the sun is 93 million miles away, how long, to the nearest day, would it take to get there travelling at 45 mph?
4. A sheep is born on 23 August 1998 and dies on 15 March 1999. For how many days, whole or part, is it alive?
5. Subtract 457 from one hundred thousand and multiply the answer by 17.

6. How many words are there in a book if it has 458 pages and an average of 321 words on each page?

7. The average age of a group of 7 children is 12 years 1 month. An additional child aged 11 years 5 months joins the group. What is the new average age of the group?

8. On Monday I spend $3.62, on Tuesday double that amount, on Wednesday double the Tuesday amount and so on until Saturday. What do I spend on Saturday?

9. It is now 0943. What was the time 1000 minutes ago?

10. Tyres cost £88.75 each. I replace all four tyres on my car every 20,000 miles. What do I spend on tyres every 160,000 miles?

Share Prices

Calculator allowed – 5 minutes

Gains last week

	% gain	end of week price
ABC clothing	14	64
PQR drinks	23	80
XYZ foods	42	180
LMN tools	11	40
IJK motors	12	582

Losses last week

	% loss	end of week price
DEF engineering	19	817
QRS transport	8	58
UVW building	28	519
STU paper	59	23
JKL sports	20	52

All percentages are to the nearest whole number.

What were the prices at the beginning of the week for the following?

1. ABC clothing	6. UVW building
2. DEF engineering	7. LMN tools
3. PQR drinks	8. STU paper
4. QRS transport	9. IJK motors
5. XYZ foods	10. JKL sports

Final Number Fun

Calculator allowed – 10 minutes

1. What are the missing digits if 34_ _81 is a perfect square?

2. A man leaves one-third of his money to this first son, one-third of the remainder to the next and so on, with the final remainder going to his only daughter. He left £16,200 and the daughter received £3200. How many sons did he have?

3. Find three consecutive numbers whose product is 1404816.

4. You can buy stamps with values 5p, 12p and 27p. What numbers of pence up to 30 can you not make using these stamps?

5. British car registrations are in the form A 123 XYZ. How many cars can be registered with numbers like this, all starting with A, having any 1-, 2- or 3-digit number and finshing with XYZ or XZY or YZX or YXZ or ZXY or ZYX?

6. During a 12-hour period. how many times are there when the hands of a clock will be exactly above one another?

7. What is the smallest number whose digits are reversed when it is multiplied by 4?

8. How many numbers less than 40 are not divisible by any of the numbers 2, 3, or 5?

9. A worker earns $12,000 per year. The salary is increased by 12%, but then the new salary is decreased by 12%. What is the final salary?

10. How many 9s are there if you write down all the numbers from 1 to 100 inclusive?

ANSWERS

| A1 | More Calculator Practice | Q43 |

1. 5213.82; 2. 2.0942558; 3. 105120; 4. 2000; 5. 5000;
6. 1.9807956; 7. 1; 8. 6.7775; 9. 4 October; 10. 0.0999

| A2 | International Paper Sizes | Q22 |

1. a.17 b.47 c.17 d.3; 2.129; 3. 700.95; 4. 1060920mm^2;
5. 35595mm; 6. 94p; 7. 1000 sheets of A1; 8. 90;
9. 89244.297cm^3; 10. 491,784,000,000mm^2

| A3 | Taxing Problems | Q39 |

1. 250; 2. 1437. 50; 3. 2687.50; 4. 3937.50; 5. 5375;
6. 395375; 7. 10335; 8. 35375; 9. 40; 10. 153375

| A4 | Rows and Columns | Q17 |

1. 955; 2. 550; 3. 55; 4. 460; 5. 5050; 6. 5050; 7. 505;
8. 505; 9. 495; 10. 495

| A5 | More Mental Practice | Q18 |

1. 47; 2. 8; 3. 72; 4. 6; 5. 87; 6. 48; 7. 276; 8. 28; 9. 370;
10. 72; 11. 1141; 12. 13; 13. 110; 14. 1625; 15. 2122;
16. 1291; 17. 102; 18. 543; 19. 718; 20. 834

| A6 | Number Pattern | Q9 |

1.0; 2. 3; 3. 4; 4. 5; 5. 6; 6. 1; 7. 7; 8. 8; 9. 2

| A7 | Numbers Everywhere | Q37 |

1. 487.5; 2. £10.93; 3. $26; 4. £115.60; 5. 18.46;
6. £526.40; 7. $322; 8. £1445; 9. 117; 10. 46.15

2	4	9	9	7	5
3	■	8	8	■	3
4	7	7	7	7	4
5	8	6	6	8	5
6	■	5	5	■	6
7	9	4	4	9	7

A9   **How Many?**   **Q16**

1. 95; 2. 31680; 3. 5280; 4. 560; 5. 12; 6. 24; 7. 8;
8. 17437; 9. 3 (11, 13, 17); 10. 31

A10   **Final Number Fun**   **Q48**

1. 349281; 2. 4; 3. 111, 112, 113; 4. 1, 2, 3, 4, 6, 7, 8, 9,
11, 13, 14, 16, 18, 19, 21, 23, 26, 28, 29; 5. 5994; 6. 12;
7. 2178; 8. 10; 9. $11827.20; 10. 20

A11   **Calculator Practice**   **Q4**

1. 7.65; 2. 33.32; 3. 76.5; 4. 2.54; 5. £385.35; 6. $348.65;
7. 1.5cm; 8. 109.98; 9. 7 hours 40 minutes; 10. 86,400

A12   **The Meeting**   **Q26**

1. One – Friday, 3 June; 2. One – Friday, 3 June; 3. None;
4. Friday and Saturday, 3–4 June; 5. Tuesday, 24 May;
6. Monday, 23 May; 7. 22; 8. 15; 9. 80%; 10. Friday,
1 July

A13	More Mental Practice	Q42

1. 127.5; 2. 3360; 3. 9990; 4. 0.00049; 5. 41; 6. 290;
7. 52.30; 8. 35250; 9. £9.03; 10. 1001

A14	Train Times	Q35

1. 2h 46m; 2. 154; 3. 4h 1m; 4. 31h 12m; 5. 1554;
6. 1525; 7. Kingsville Pullman, 11 minutes; 8. 24
minutes; 9. 19.8 minutes; 10. 1543, 555 minutes

A15	Numbers and Measures	Q19

1. 1.25; 2. 8.75; 3. 1950; 4. 6.2; 5. 7.45; 6. 36; 7. 110;
8. 10.5; 9. 13.75; 10. 6.12; 11. 40; 12. 12660; 13. 21080;
14. 2300; 15. 3080; 16. 7.2; 17. 430; 18. 12.8%;
19. a. £136.80; b. £3.60; c. £43.20; d. £7558.20 and
£145.35

A16	Mental Practice 1	Q1

1. 145; 2. 69; 3. 102; 4. 45; 5. 270; 6. 600; 7. 360; 8. 40;
9. 92; 10. 5 hours

A17	Quick Sums	Q15

1. 101088; 2. 78455; 3. 23.3712; 4. 3.73103; 5. 101.088;
6. 78.445; 7. 88891; 8. 18.35613; 9. 479.52; 10. 8.06216

A18	More Numbers	Q28

1. d; 2. d; 3. a; 4. c; 5. b; 6. d; 7. c; 8. b; 9. e; 10. e

A19   Windows, Golf Balls, CDs & Bestwood House   Q38

1. $237.50; 2. 56; 3. 48; 4. 10; 5. 57p; 6. 56; 7. £7.64;
8. £228.75; 9. 23.5%; 10. 12

A20   Mental Practice 2   Q2

1. $3.54; 2. 7; 3. 59.5; 4. 66.66666; 5. 0.0003; 6. 31;
7. 400; 8. 0621; 9. 60 cents; 10. 41

A21   A Pack of Cards   Q31

1. 216; 2. 30.77%; 3. 364; 4. 15.38%; 5. 15.38%;
6. 7.70%; 7. 3840; 8. 945; 9. highest 92, lowest 28;
10. 624cm^2

A22   Number Miscellany   Q46

1. 496; 2. 650; 3. 86,111 days; 4. 205; 5. 1,692,231;
6. 147,018; 7. 12 years 0 months; 8. $115.84; 9. 17.03;
10. £2840

A23   A Stay in a Hotel   Q34

1. £329.40; 2. £47.60; 3. £1815.10; 4. 19.3%; 5. 23%;
6. £3515.20; 7. $340.38; 8. £2560.20; 9. £256.40;
10. £86,268

A24   Percentages   Q8

1. b; 2. b; 3. c; 4. c; 5. d; 6. a; 7. b; 8. c; 9. c; 10. d

A25   Numbers   Q27

1. d; 2. c; 3. c; 4. b; 5. d; 6. e; 7. e; 8. d; 9. c; 10. a

1. 10 minutes; 2. 28 hours 34 minutes; 3. 12 hours 24 minutes; 4. 13 hours 30 minutes; 5. 50 hours; 6. 72; 7. 240; 8. 432; 9. 240; 10. 4200

4	9	7	7	■	6
4	■	2	9	5	0
9	5	0	■	6	4
9	9	■	6	7	8
9	9	9	9	■	0
9	■	3	2	1	0

A	5264	Y
E	6272	O
G	5880	U
H	280	H
I	840	A
O	6440	V
O	4760	E
T	336	G
T	4928	O
U	672	T
V	5320	I
Y	5936	T

A29	Train Fares	Q44

1. 31; 2. 189; 3. 77; 4. 77; 5. 151; 6. 109; 7. 107; 8. 146;
9. 64; 10. 240

A30	Ages	Q11

1. 315; 2. 99; 3. 1269; 4. 50995; 5. 10; 6. 35.5; 7. 55;
8. 37; 9. 2011; 10. 2034

A31	Mental Practice 3	Q3

1. 22; 2. £4.75; 3. 1200; 4. 10; 5. 12.5 ; 6. 6.7; 7. 0.17;
8. 23; 9. 6 hours; 10. 35,000

A32	Telephones	Q30

1. £72; 2. £107.27; 3. 20; 4. £105.60; 5. £30.13;
6. £1127.28; 7. C by £5; 8. £49.75; 9. £19.25;
10. £415.38

A33	Another Number Pattern	Q12

1. 16; 2. 323192; 3. 56; 4. 356; 5. 612; 6. 392; 7. 111;
8. 918; 9. 222; 10. 29

A34	Share Prices	Q47

1. 56; 2. 1009; 3. 65; 4. 63; 5. 127; 6. 721; 7. 36; 8. 56;
9. 520; 10. 65

A35	The Race	Q5

1. 13; 2. 229; 3. 34m 24s; 4. 9; 5. 12m 45s; 6. 669;
7. 171; 8. 3; 9. 7; 10. 4

A36   Numbers in a Day   Q36

1. 967; 2. 43; 3. 23.28; 4. 6.25%; 5. 18; 6. £10.90; 7. 201;
8. £1014; 9. 285; 10. 32

A37   Biggest and Smallest   Q10

1. 83; 2. 27; 3. 4115; 4. 7; 5. 20; 6. 15; 7. 2556; 8. 774;
9. 26; 10. 84

A38   Palindromic Numbers   Q45

1. 137731; 2. 1991 + 2002 = 3993;
3. 11 + 22 + 33 + 44 + 55 + 66 + 77 + 88 + 99 = 495;
4. 4040404; 5. 121815.12; 6. 654456; 7. 824424;
8. 19322391; 9. 12344321; 10. 99899899

A39   International Air Distances   Q21

1. 5770; 2. 10,522; 3. 361,192; 4. 10; 5. 142,104;
6. a. $267.60 b. $702 c. $909.90; 7. 288; 8. 5007.6;
9. £135.60; 10. $0.42

A40   Shares, Savings, Daylight & Walking   Q40

1. 118; 2. $1885; 3. 877; 4. 100%; 5. 43m 13.5s; 6. 30%;
7. 241; 8. 2400; 9. 332; 10. $162.50

A41	Spring Folly?	Q25

1.	1	A
2.	16	P
3.	18	R
4.	9	I
5.	12	L
6.	6	F
7.	15	O
8.	15	O
9.	12	L

A42	Some Quick Percentages	Q7

1. 34131; 2. 32697; 3. 21503; 4. 30881; 5. 24167;
6. 14335; 7. 2%; 8. 2%; 9. 3%; 10. 84377

A43	House Numbers	Q23

1. 788; 2. 100; 3. 102, 123; 4. 9; 5. 190 metres; 6. 1995
metres; 7. 492; 8. 132; 9. 138; 10. 29,563

A44	Four Numbers	Q33

1. 2592/5184/10368/10368/20736/41472; 2. 90720;
3. 1296/5184/20736/82944; 4. 110160; 5. 12.5; 6. 570;
7. 480; 8. 45; 9. 9; 10. 77

A45	Hotels	Q41

1. £2344; 2. £5823.50; 3. £1966; 4. 354; 5. £906;
6. £2770.20; 7. 6; 8. £7808; 9. £7760; 10. £8111

1. 70; 2. 29 July; 3. 7 seconds; 4. 4; 5. 61; 6. 31; 7. 51, 52, 53; 8. 113, 114, 115; 9. 5 hours 20 minutes; 10. 421

1. 1500 on 5 April; 2. 2215 on 8 March; 3. 0947; 4. 2150; 5. Kuwait 1247; New York 0447; 6. 1258 on 14 May; 7. 1940 on 28 February; 8. 0200; 9. 0817; 10. 1617

A	1				
B	2	6			
C	3	7	3		
D	4	8	2	5	
E	5	9	1	4	6
F	6	4	1	9	5
G	5	2	7	4	
H	3	8	3		
I	6	2			
J	1				

PERSONAL RECORD OF SCORES

Keep a record of your scores and times. Not only should you get quicker with practice but you should also be achieving higher scores.

Any score of 80 per cent or more is good. Anything less than 40 per cent is an indication that you need to practise more!

	1st attempt Score Time	2nd attempt Score Time	3rd attempt Score Time
Question 1			
Question 2			
Question 3			
Question 4			
Question 5			
Question 6			
Question 7			
Question 8			
Question 9			
Question 10			
Question 11			
Question 12			
Question 13			
Question 14			
Question 15			

	1st attempt		2nd attempt		3rd attempt	
	Score	Time	Score	Time	Score	Time
Question 16						
Question 17						
Question 18						
Question 19						
Question 20						
Question 21						
Question 22						
Question 23						
Question 24						
Question 25						
Question 26						
Question 27						
Question 28						
Question 29						
Question 30						
Question 31						
Question 32						
Question 33						
Question 34						
Question 35						
Question 36						
Question 37						
Question 38						
Question 39						
Question 40						

	1st attempt Score Time	2nd attempt Score Time	3rd attempt Score Time
Question 41			
Question 42			
Question 43			
Question 44			
Question 45			
Question 46			
Question 47			
Question 48			

NUMBERS CAN BE INTERESTING

Numbers have many fascinating properties, and they often produce unexpected patterns. As relaxation after the puzzles you might like to consider some of the following. If you do, you will almost certainly find that you are improving your skill and confidence with numbers at the same time.

Odd Numbers

Write down a list of the first 20 odd numbers. Write down a list of the totals you get when you add:

the first two numbers in the list

the first three

the first four, and so on

What do you notice about the answers?

Quick Addition!

The famous mathematician Carl Friedrich Gauss lived from 1777 to 1855. There is a story that when he was a pupil at school the teacher told him to add up the whole numbers from 1 to 100 as a punishment. To the teacher's surprise, Carl gave the answer in a few seconds.

The correct answer is 5050. Can you find a quick way of getting it without having to add all the individual numbers?

Elevens can be Interesting

Look at the following:

1x11=11

11x11=121

111x111=12321

What pattern do you notice? Does the pattern continue? Can you explain why it works?

The Same Answer Every Time

Choose any three-digit number – 745, for example – and reverse the digits to get 547. Find the difference between the two numbers – 745 - 547 = 198.

Reverse the digits again and add the last two numbers – 198 + 891. What do you get?

Try again with some different numbers. What happens?

How Many Numbers are Perfect

The factors of a number are those numbers that will divide exactly into it – for example, 16 has factors 1, 2, 4 and 8, and 36 has factors 1, 2, 3, 4, 6, 9, 12 and 18.

If the factors of a number add up to the number itself, it is called a perfect number. Therefore:

1 is perfect

6 is perfect (since its factors are 1, 2 and 3)

8 is not perfect

Can you find any more perfect numbers after 1 and 6?

The Famous Four 4s

There is a famous problem that requires numbers to be made using exactly four 4s and normal mathematical notation. For example, $1 = 44/44$, $2 = 4/4 + 4/4$, $3 = (4+4+4)/4$ and so on.

How many numbers from 1 to 100 can you make this way?

Try the same problem with seven 7s and five 5s.

Arrangements

In how many ways can you arrange two books on a shelf?

Clearly the answer is 2.

What about three books? Then four books? Five books?

Can you find a pattern? Could you predict the number of ways for 20 books?

Try using your own books if you get stuck, but take care – you may be arranging books for quite a long time!

Magic Squares

Can you place the numbers 1, 2, 3, 4, 5, 6, 7, 8 and 9 in the grid so that the three rows, the three columns and the two diagonals all add up to the same total?

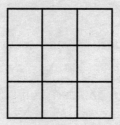

Can you do the same using this grid with the numbers 1, 2, 3, 4, 5, 6, 7, 8, 9, 10, 11, 12, 13, 14, 15 and 16?

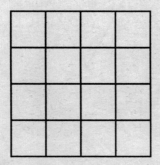

The Marvellous 26 Puzzle

Can you insert the numbers 1, 2, 3, 4, 5, 6, 7, 8, 9, 10, 11 and 12 in the circles so that the rows of numbers along the sides of each triangle (6 of them) all add up to 26 and the six numbers around the central hexagon also add up to 26?

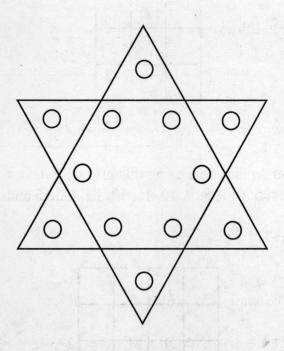

ANSWERS AND NOTES

Odd Numbers

Addition of odd numbers gives square numbers.
Thus $1 + 3 = 4 = 2^2$, $1 + 3 + 5 = 9 = 3^2$,
$1+3+5+7 = 16 = 4^2$ and so on. In general, if the first n odd numbers are added, the sum is n^2.

Quick Addition

$1 + 2 + 3 + 4 + \ldots + 98 + 99 + 100$ can be written as

$$1 \ + \ 2 \ + \ 3 \ + \ 4 \ + \ldots \ + 49 \ + 50$$
$$+100 \ + 99 \ + 98 \ + 97 \ + \ldots \ + 52 \ + 51$$

and each vertical pair of numbers adds up to 101 giving a total of $50 \times 101 = 5050$

In general, if the first n numbers are added, the sum is:

$$\frac{n(n+1)}{2}$$

so, for example, if $n = 50$

$$\frac{n(n+1)}{2} \ = \frac{50 \times 51}{2} \ = 1275$$

and so the sum of the first 50 numbers is 1275.

Elevens can be Interesting

The pattern does continue. For example
$111111 \times 111111 = 12345654321$. If the sum is written
as a 'long multiplication' it becomes clear why this
pattern occurs and why it will break down when there
are ten 1s or more (although the answers still produce
some interesting patterns).

The Same Answer Every Time

With all starting numbers (unless the first and last
digit are the same) the answer is 1089. For example

$$
\begin{array}{r}
621 \\
-126 \\
\hline
495 \\
+594 \\
\hline
1089
\end{array}
$$

If the first and last digits are the same – 626, for
example – then the first subtration will give zero. If
the first and last digits differ by one – 625, for
example – a zero needs to be written in front of the
first subtraction

$$
\begin{array}{r}
625 \\
-526 \\
\hline
099 \\
+990 \\
\hline
1089
\end{array}
$$

How Many Numbers are Perfect?

The Greeks believed perfect numbers had a mystical property. It took six days for the Creation and there are 28 days in a lunar month (28 being the next perfect number). After 6 the next perfect numbers are 28, 496, 8128, 3355036.

The Famous Four 4s

The solution depends on what notation is allowed. With 'ordinary' notation – addition, subtraction, division, multiplication and decimal points – you can get up to 22; if the square root sign is allowed, up to 30 and if factorials are allowed, up to 112.

Arrangements

Three books can be arranged in six ways; four books can be arranged in 24 ways; five books can be arranged in 120 ways and so on. In general, n books can be arranged in n! ways where $n! = 1 \times 2 \times 3 \times 4 \times 5 \times 6 \times \ldots \ldots \times (n-1) \times n$.

So 20 books can be arranged in 20! ways where $20! = 1 \times 2 \times 3 \times 4 \times 5 \times 6 \times 7 \times 8 \times 9 \times 10 \times 11 \times 12 \times 13 \times 14 \times 15 \times 16 \times 17 \times 18 \times 19 \times 20$ which is approximately 24,000,000,000,000,000,000

Magic Squares
Possible solutions

8	1	6
3	5	7
4	9	2

16	3	2	13
5	10	11	8
9	6	7	12
4	15	14	1

For a 5 × 5 square a possible solution is

17	24	1	8	15
23	5	7	14	16
4	6	13	20	22
10	12	19	21	3
11	18	25	2	9

The Marvellous 26 Puzzle
One solution is

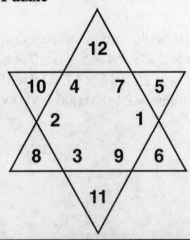

112